BIG ORANGE COUNTRY®

T

THE MOST SPECTACULAR SIGHTS & SOUNDS OF TENNESSEE FOOTBALL

BIG ORANGE COUNTRY®

Ⓣ

THE MOST SPECTACULAR SIGHTS & SOUNDS OF TENNESSEE FOOTBALL

ATHLON® SPORTS™

RUTLEDGE HILL PRESS™
NASHVILLE, TENNESSEE

A DIVISION OF THOMAS NELSON PUBLISHERS, INC.
WWW.THOMASNELSON.COM

Published by Rutledge Hill Press, a Division of Thomas Nelson, Inc., P.O. Box 141000, Nashville, Tennessee, 37214.

1-4016-0101-4

Printed in the United States of America
03 04 05 06 07—5 4 3 2 1

TABLE OF CONTENTS

ACKNOWLEDGMENTS

Athlon Sports would like to thank Rutledge Hill Press, Kevin Daniels, Tim Clark, the College Football Hall of Fame, the University of Tennessee Sports Information office, the Pride of the Southland Band, and above all the Tennessee fans, whose passionate devotion to their Volunteers defines what college football is all about. Audio highlights compliments of Host Communications and Vol Radio Network.

INTRODUCTION

The images are unforgettable and too numerous to count.

The orange-clad Volunteers bursting through the T as more than 100,000 citizens of Vol Nation roar themselves hoarse. Phillip Fulmer and the 1998 Vols hoisting the championship hardware. Peyton Manning leading the Pride of the Southland Band in the playing of Rocky Top after his final regular-season game.

Condredge Holloway slithering his way through impossibly small openings in the defense on his way to paydirt. John Ward marking off the yardage on another touchdown run before exclaiming, "Give . . . him . . . six!" Dewey Warren to Richmond Flowers. Hank Lauricella, Doug Atkins, Gene McEver. General Neyland.

In this book, we've attempted to distill the pageantry and drama of Tennessee football into the pages that follow. It's a daunting task. No program in the country inspires the loyalty and passion that Tennessee football exacts from its fans. And with good reason.

Through the words, images and sounds we present here, you can get a taste of what Tennessee football is all about. If you're a true Tennessee fan, we can guarantee a few goose bumps by the time you're finished

So let's get started. As has been said many times over: "It's football time in Tennessee!"

TRADITIONS AND PAGEANTRY

The traditions and pageantry of Tennessee football are rich and deep. They are passed down from generation to generation: a sense of duty, Southern pride, and, of course, an undying love for Tennessee football.

ORANGE AND WHITE

The same year Tennessee played its first football game—a 24–0 loss to Sewanee in 1891—the school adopted orange and white as its official colors to reflect the color of the American daisies that grow in profusion on The Hill. But the Volunteers wore black jerseys until 1922, when they changed to orange at the instigation of team captain Roy "Pap" Striegel.

THE VOLUNTEER NAVY

In a maneuver aimed at getting around the maddening gameday traffic in Knoxville, former Tennessee broadcaster George Mooney arrived by boat on the Tennessee River for a game in 1962 and docked on the bank near the stadium. It was an idea whose time had come. It quickly caught on, and thus was born the Volunteer Navy, a floating tailgate party that crowds the Tennessee River in the shadow of Neyland Stadium.

VOL WALK

As players and coaches make their way from the football complex to the stadium before each home game, they are greeted by thousands of cheering fans in what has taken on a traditional life of its own as the Vol Walk. It's a chill-inducing experience for players, coaches and fans alike.

RUNNING THROUGH THE T

At game time, the Pride of the Southland Band forms a Block T on Shields-Watkins Field, from end line to sideline. The team emerges from the tunnel and runs through the T to the cheers of 100,000-plus Vol faithful. It's one of the great moments in all of college football.

CHECKERBOARD END ZONES

The orange and white checkerboard end zones first appeared in 1964, the first year of current athletic director Doug Dickey's coaching tenure. They disappeared in 1968 with the introduction of an artificial playing surface, then reappeared in 1989 and remain there to this day.

NEYLAND STADIUM

What began in 1921 as Shields-Watkins Field, capacity 3,200, has grown into 104,079-seat Neyland Stadium, one of only three football facilities in the nation with 100,000-plus seating capacity. Upon the death in 1962 of immortal coach Bob Neyland, the stadium was rededicated in his honor.

VOLUNTEERS

Tennessee became known as the Volunteer State in the 1800s as a result of the willingness of Tennesseans to volunteer for military service in defense of their country. At the outbreak of the War of 1812, a call was issued for 3,500 Tennessee men, and 25,000 answered the call. The reputation of Tennesseans' fighting spirit was further strengthened in the Mexican War. Hence the nickname—Volunteers.

SMOKEY THE BLUE TICK HOUND

Serving as mascot for the Volunteer football team since 1953 is Smokey the blue tick coon hound. The late Rev. Bill Brooks' prize winner served as Smokey I in 1953 and '54. The Tennessee-bred canine currently leading the Vols through the T prior to each home game and stalking the sidelines is Smokey VIII.

THE PRIDE OF THE SOUTHLAND BAND

The football team provides most of the entertainment on football Saturdays in Knoxville, but not all of it. The University of Tennessee's Pride of the Southland Band is one of the most prestigious marching bands in all the land. Prior to each home game, the 330-member organization marches from the Stokely Athletic Center down Volunteer Boulevard, stopping for periodic renditions of Rocky Top, before making its way into Neyland Stadium. The pregame T and the halftime performances lend pageantry to the proceedings. The "Pride" has also appeared at over 40 bowl games and the last 10 presidential inaugurations.

HERE'S TO OLD TENNESSEE
(DOWN THE FIELD)

HERE'S TO OLD TENNESSEE

NE'ER SHALL WE SEVER

WE PLEDGE OUR LOYALTY

FOR EVER AND EVER

BACKING HER FOOTBALL TEAM

FALTERING NEVER

CHEER AND FIGHT WITH ALL YOUR MIGHT

FOR TENNESSEE!

ROCKY TOP

Wish that I was on ol' Rocky Top
Down in the Tennessee hills;
Ain't no smoggy smoke on Rocky Top,
Ain't no telephone bills.
Once I had a girl on Rocky Top,
Half bear, other half cat;
Wild as a mink but sweet as soda pop,
I still dream about that.

Rocky Top, you'll always be
Home sweet home to me;
Good ol' Rocky Top —
Rocky Top Tennessee, Rocky Top Tennessee

Once two strangers climbed ol' Rocky Top,
Lookin' for a moonshine still;
Strangers ain't come down from Rocky Top,
Reckon they never will.
Corn won't grow at all on Rocky Top,
Dirt's too rocky by far;
That's why all the folks on Rocky Top
Get their corn from a jar.

(REFRAIN)

I've had years of cramped-up city life,
Trapped like a duck in a pen;
All I know is it's a pity life
Can't be simple again.

(REFRAIN)

ALMA MATER

On a hallowed hill in Tennessee
Like a beacon shining bright
The stately walls of old UT
Rise glorious to the sight.

(REFRAIN)

So here's to you, old Tennessee
Our alma mater true.
We pledge in love and harmony
Our loyalty to you.

What torches kindled at that flame
Have passed from hand to hand.
What hearts cemented in that name
Bind land to stranger land.

(REFRAIN)

O, ever as we strive to rise
On life's unresting stream
Dear Alma Mater, may our eyes
Be lifted to that gleam.

(REFRAIN)

GREAT TEAMS

The 1951 and 1998 National Championship teams certainly weren't the only great teams in Vol history. Here's a quick sampling of some of the other great units to grace The Hill.

1914 (9–0)

Had there been wire service polls in 1914, coach Zora Clevenger's 1914 Tennessee team might have been National Champs. Previous to that season, UT had been winless against Vanderbilt in 12 tries, but the Vols pulled off a 16–14 win in Nashville that year on the way to a perfect 9–0 slate, outscoring their opponents by a total of 374–37. Tennessee captured its first championship in football that season, finishing atop the Southern Intercollegiate Athletic Association standings.

1916 (8–0–1)

John R. Bender took over as Tennessee coach in 1916 and finished the year undefeated, though a scoreless tie with Kentucky in the season finale marred the record. As a result, the SIAA title was awarded to Georgia Tech. A 16–6 win over Vanderbilt brought UT's record against its cross-state rival to 2–12–1.

1938 (11−0), 1939 (10−1), 1940 (10−1)

From 1938 through 1940, Bob Neyland's Tennessee teams enjoyed three straight perfect regular seasons. From midseason 1938 until midseason 1940, the Vols didn't surrender a regular-season point. The 1939 Tennessee team is the last in college football history to finish a regular season unscored-upon. The record over those three years, counting bowl games: 31−2.

1950 (11−1)

The Big Orange posted a 10−1 regular-season mark in 1950, dropping only Game 2 to Mississippi State. The biggest win of the year was a 7−0 decision over Bear Bryant's undefeated and top-ranked Kentucky team, featuring SEC Player of the Year Babe Parilli at quarterback, on November 25. The Vols went on to upset Texas 20−14 in the Cotton Bowl, keyed by a scintillating 75-yard run by Hank Lauricella. Two of the three teams ranked ahead of Tennessee—Oklahoma and Texas—lost their Bowl games, and second-ranked Army had lost to Navy on December 2. But the polls were closed.

1951 (10—1)

Tennessee's first consensus National Championship came in the second-to-last year of Bob Neyland's coaching tenure. The 1951 Vols featured tailback Hank Lauricella, who finished second in that year's Heisman voting, and Doug Atkins, arguably the greatest defensive end who ever played the game. UT outscored its opponents 386—116 and finished the regular season 10—0 before dropping the Sugar Bowl to Maryland 28—13.

1956 (10—1)

With former Vol end and Hall of Fame coach Bowden Wyatt in his second season at the helm in Knoxville, Tennessee won the 1956 SEC Championship with a 10—0 regular-season record before dropping the Sugar Bowl to Baylor 13—7. The Vols' 6—0 win over Georgia Tech that year is an all-time college football classic. Tailback Johnny Majors finished second in the Heisman voting, and Tennessee finished second nationally in the final rankings.

1967 (9 – 2)

The 1967 Volunteers, with All-Americans in center Bob Johnson and wingback Richmond Flowers, won the SEC and a share of the National Championship. In between losses to UCLA and Heisman Trophy winner Gary Beban in the opener and to third-ranked Oklahoma in the Orange Bowl, the Vols were perfect. The highlight of the season was a 23–14 win at Alabama, ending a six-year string of futility against the Tide.

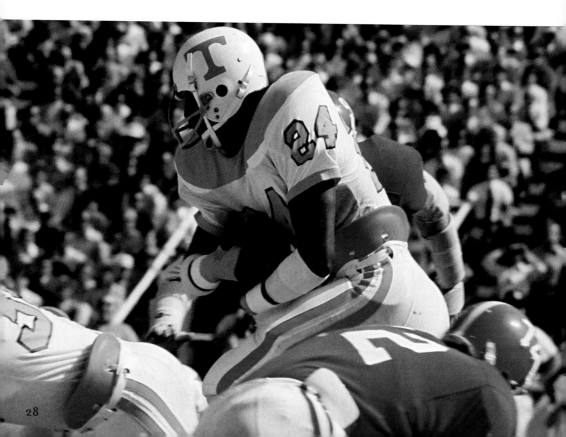

1970 (11-1)

The Volunteers finished with a fourth-place national ranking in 1970, Bill Battle's inaugural season as head coach. The only smudge on the record was a three-point loss to Auburn in Game 2. Guard Chip Kell, defensive back Bobby Majors and linebacker Jackie Walker were All-Americans. The season was capped by a 34–13 rout of Air Force in the Sugar Bowl.

1985 (9-1-2)

One of the most beloved teams in Tennessee history, the 1985 squad overcame a midseason injury to quarterback Tony Robinson to earn the SEC title on pure grit and character. An early-season rout of Auburn and the Vols' fourth straight win over Alabama keyed the title run, which put the Vols in the Sugar Bowl against heavily favored Miami. On a magical night in New Orleans, Tennessee stuffed Vinny Testaverde and the Hurricanes 35–7 to complete one of the great seasons in Volunteer annals.

1989 (11-1)

The Vols won the second of coach Johnny Majors' three SEC Championships and ranked fifth in the final wire service polls with an 11–1 campaign in 1989. The only setback was a 47–30 shootout at Alabama. Antone Davis and All-American Eric Still were the most dominating guard duo in Knoxville since Bob Suffridge and Ed Molinski in the glory years of 1938–40. Chuck Webb rushed for 1,236 yards at a hair under six per carry and added 250 rushing yards in a 31–27 Cotton Bowl victory over Southwest Conference champion Arkansas.

1 9 9 8 (1 3 - 0)

Tennessee posted its second consensus National Championship, and sixth overall, in 1998. Tee Martin took over for the graduated Peyton Manning at quarterback and led his team to the promised land. Tailback Jamal Lewis was lost for the season with a knee injury in Game 4, but Travis Henry answered the challenge and finished the season just 30 yards shy of a 1,000-yard rushing campaign. Wide receiver Peerless Price contributed 61 pass receptions to the cause. Linebackers Al Wilson and Raynoch Thompson cemented the defense, with placekicker Jeff Hall becoming the SEC's all-time leading scorer. It took three fourth-quarter rallies to finish the regular season unscathed, but these Vols were on a mission. After a resounding 23–16 victory over Florida State in the Fiesta Bowl, Tennessee stood at 13–0 and undisputed National Champion.

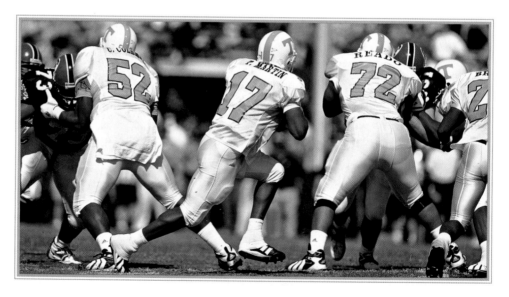

VOLS IN THE COLLEGE FOOTBALL HALL OF FAME

NATHAN DOUGHERTY (GUARD 1906–09)

INDUCTED 1967

A 6'2", 185-pound guard, Dougherty was nicknamed "The Big One." He played fullback part-time and scored a touchdown in UT's 15–0 win over Georgia in 1907. He also returned a kickoff for a touchdown in 1908. He was two-year All-Southern and team captain in 1909. Later, as chairman of Tennessee's Athletic Council, Dougherty was responsible for bringing Bob Neyland to Knoxville as head coach.

GENE McEVER (HALFBACK 1928–29, 31)

INDUCTED 1954

McEver was the personification of power football in his day. Stocky, strong and fast, he was nicknamed "The Wild Bull." McEver was a unanimous All-America halfback for three years—1928, 29 and 31. (Knee surgery kept him sidelined for 1930.) In 1929, he led all of college football in scoring with 130 points. His 98-yard kickoff return against Alabama in 1928 helped thrust the Vols into the nation's consciousness.

BEATTIE FEATHERS (HALFBACK 1931–33)

INDUCTED 1955

A halfback on Neyland's great teams of the early '30s, William Beattie Feathers seemed to fly through opposing defenses. He was a threat to score from anywhere on the field. In Tennessee's 7–3 win over Alabama in 1932, he averaged 48 yards on 21 punts and ran for the game's only touchdown. He was the SEC MVP and All-America in 1933. As a halfback with the Chicago Bears in 1934, Feathers set an NFL single-season record with 8.4 yards per carry, a mark that still stands.

COACH BOB NEYLAND (COACH 1926–1952)

INDUCTED 1956

General Robert Reese Neyland is universally recognized as one of the greatest coaches in the history of American football. It was Neyland who put Tennessee on the college football map to stay. In his 21 years at the helm (1926–1952, interrupted twice by stints of military service), Neyland compiled a record of 173–31–12. His winning percentage of .829 ranks seventh all-time in Division I-A. During one seven-year span his teams went 61–2–5. He won seven conference championships — two Southern and five SEC — and at least a share of three national titles. And in 1956, he was inducted into the College Football Hall of Fame.

Coach Neyland's legendary 7 Maxims of Football were written decades ago but are timeless bits of wisdom that still apply to Tennessee football today:

1. The team that makes the fewest mistakes will win.
2. Play for and make the breaks, and when one comes your way — SCORE.
3. If at first the game — or the breaks — go against you, don't let up . . . put on more steam.
4. Protect our kickers, our quarterback, our lead and our ballgame.
5. Ball, oskie, cover, block, cut and slice, pursue and gang tackle . . . for this is the WINNING EDGE.
6. Press the kicking game. Here is where the breaks are made.
7. Carry the fight to our opponent and keep it there for 60 minutes.

HERMAN HICKMAN (GUARD 1929–31)

INDUCTED 1959

Up through his playing days at Tennessee (1929–31), Herman Hickman ranked with Yale's Pudge Heffelfinger as the greatest guards ever to play the game. Hickman's legendary speed, power and agility made him the most famous lineman in Southern football. He could outrun almost all of his teammates. He was a human road grader on offense, and on defense he left opposing blockers and ball carriers together in heaps on the ground. After playing professionally for three years, Hickman later went on to coach at both Army and Yale.

BOBBY DODD (QUARTERBACK 1928–30)

INDUCTED 1959 (PLAYER) 1993 (COACH)

As the quarterback of Tennessee's famous Hack, Mack and Dodd backfield of 1928–30, Bobby Dodd guided the Vols to a 27–1–2 record and made All-America in 1930. Like his coach, Bob Neyland, Dodd has a stadium named after him—at Georgia Tech, where he was head coach for 22 years (1945–66) and won 71 percent of his games. Dodd is one of only three men enshrined in the College Football Hall of Fame as both a player and a coach.

BOB SUFFRIDGE (GUARD 1938–40)

INDUCTED 1961

Bob Suffridge is the only three-time consensus All-American in Tennessee history. With Suffridge at guard, the Vols plowed through three straight regular-season slates without a loss. Not particularly big for a guard (6'1", 185 lb.) even in his day, Suffridge's charge has been compared to the thrust of a jet engine. According to Neyland: "Suff had the quickest and most powerful defensive charge of any lineman I've ever seen. He never made a bad play." He was arguably the best-ever of the pulling single-wing guards.

GEORGE CAFEGO (TAILBACK 1937–39)

INDUCTED 1969

George "Bad News" Cafego was a two-year All-America single-wing tailback for some of Neyland's greatest teams. Of Cafego, the immortal coach remarked: "In practice he couldn't do anything right. But for two hours on Saturday afternoons he did everything an All-American is supposed to do." Cafego's powerful, churning legs made him hard to bring down. He also possessed blinding speed and was a deadly accurate passer. Cafego was the SEC Player of the Year in 1938 when the Volunteers went 11–0. Later in life Cafego spent 30 years as an assistant football coach at his alma mater.

BOWDEN WYATT (END 1936–38)

INDUCTED 1972 (PLAYER) 1997 (COACH)

As a senior in 1938, Bowden Wyatt was captain of the 11–0 Tennessee squad. He was an All-SEC and All-America end that year in addition to his duties as placekicker. He went on to an illustrious head coaching career at Wyoming, Arkansas and Tennessee. Along with Amos Alonzo Stagg and fellow Vol Bobby Dodd, Wyatt ranks as one of just three men in the College Football Hall of Fame as both a player and a coach.

ED MOLINSKI (GUARD 1938–40)

INDUCTED 1990

Molinski teamed with Bob Suffridge to form possibly the top guard combo of all time through the halcyon days of 1938, '39 and '40. He was a key to the Tennessee defense that made shutouts a regular occurrence, including the unscored-upon unit of 1939. Molinski was All-SEC and All-America in 1939 and '40.

HANK LAURICELLA (TAILBACK 1949–51)

INDUCTED 1981

Lauricella, a New Orleans native, was an All-SEC selection in 1950 and an All-American in 1951, when he finished as runner-up in the Heisman voting behind Princeton's Dick Kazmaier. Lauricella was the ultimate single-wing tailback—a position made famous at UT during Neyland's tenure. Lauricella's shining moment as a Vol came in the 1951 Cotton Bowl game when he weaved through the Texas defense for 75 yards to set up the first touchdown of the day in the Vols' 20–14 victory. He then proceeded to lead Tennessee to its first consensus National Title the following season.

JOHN MICHELS (GUARD 1950–52)

INDUCTED 1996

John Michels may be overshadowed by the likes of Suffridge, Molinski, Dougherty and Hickman as UT guards, but as a blocker he took a back seat to none. He was All-SEC in 1951 and All-America in '52. Tennessee won 27 of 32 games with Michels in the lineup. He later went on to a career as an assistant coach in the NFL. He was on the staff of the Minnesota Vikings for 27 years, including four Super Bowl campaigns.

DOUG ATKINS (END 1950–52)

INDUCTED 1985

If Doug Atkins isn't the scariest defensive end ever to play organized football, he is certainly in the top three. He was All-SEC in 1951, All-America in 1952 and the first-round draft pick of the Chicago Bears in 1953. Atkins was voted the SEC Player of the Quarter Century (1950–74) by the Football Writers Association. He is the only UT Vol in both the College and Pro Football Halls of Fame.

JOHNNY MAJORS (TAILBACK 1954–56)

INDUCTED 1987

Johnny Majors finished second in the Heisman voting after leading Tennessee to a 10–1 record in 1956. (Paul Hornung of 2–8 Notre Dame won it.) Through his career, Majors led the Vols in passing, rushing, scoring, punting, punt returns and kickoff returns. He was a two-time SEC Player of the Year in 1955 and '56. After his playing career, Majors held head coaching offices at Iowa State, Pittsburgh and UT, winning a National Title in 1976 at Pitt.

BOB JOHNSON (CENTER 1965–67)

INDUCTED 1989

Bob Johnson was a two-time All-America center for Tennessee in 1966 and '67, captaining coach Doug Dickey's '67 squad that won a share of the National Championship. A member of the SEC All-Quarter Century team, Johnson also was an Academic All-American and recipient of the National Football Foundation Post-Graduate Scholarship in 1967. He was the first overall NFL Draft choice in 1968, taken by the expansion Cincinnati Bengals.

STEVE DeLONG (MIDDLE GUARD 1962–64)

INDUCTED 1993

Steve DeLong was a two-time All-American in 1963 and 1964 and team captain in '64. Tennessee's football fortunes were on a down cycle in DeLong's senior year, but that didn't deter the Norfolk, Virginia, native from dominating games at his middle guard position. He took home the Outland Trophy as the nation's best interior lineman and was a first-round draft pick in 1965.

STEVE KINER (LINEBACKER 1967–69)

INDUCTED 1999

Bear Bryant once compared Steve Kiner to former Bama great Lee Roy Jordan. Kiner was one of the finest linebackers the SEC ever produced. The conference's Sophomore of the Year in 1967, Kiner was an All-American in 1968 and '69. He possessed more speed than most running backs and was the toughest linebacker in the game during his day.

REGGIE WHITE (DEFENSIVE TACKLE 1980–83)

INDUCTED 2002

It might require a knowledge of history to recognize the names of some of Tennessee's Hall of Famers, but anybody who is old enough to drive a car and vote knows Reggie White, the Vols' latest inductee. The Minister of Defense holds school records for sacks in a single season with 15 in 1983 and in a career with 32. He holds the NFL record for career sacks with 192.5. In 1983, White was the SEC Player of the Year and an All-American.

Other Tennessee Greats

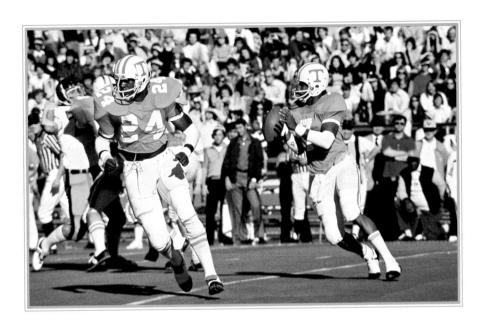

CONDREDGE HOLLOWAY (QUARTERBACK 1972–74)

Condredge Holloway threw for well over 3,000 yards as a quarterback at Tennessee, and he may even be better remembered as a dazzling open-field runner. But his greatest legacy is the one he left as the first black quarterback in the history of the Southeastern Conference. Holloway also was a gifted baseball player, having turned down a lucrative offer from the Montreal Expos to remain at UT. After graduation, Holloway enjoyed a long and successful career in the Canadian Football League.

PEYTON MANNING (QUARTERBACK 1994–97)

Peyton Manning's return home from the Downtown Athletic Club without the 1997 Heisman Trophy was hard to figure. He had just led the Vols to an 11–2 record and the SEC title. He finished his career having rewritten the school passing record book and extensively edited the SEC records. He left Knoxville in possession of conference marks for career wins as a starter, completions, completion percentage, passing yards and total offense, among others. He held NCAA records for lowest interception percentage for a season and career, and ranked third in NCAA history in passing yards and total offense. He won the 1997 Davey O'Brien and Johnny Unitas Awards, and he was the SEC Player of the Year and a unanimous All-American.

JOHN HENDERSON (DEFENSIVE TACKLE 1999–2001)

John Henderson brought the 2000 Outland Trophy home to Tennessee, and was a finalist for the 2001 hardware despit being hobbled by a sprained ankle all season and missing two games. In 2000, his second year as a starter, the Nashville native recorded 71 tackles and 12 sacks, forced four fumbles and recovered three. He added another 39 stops and 4.5 sacks during his injury-shortened 2001 campaign. Big John was a two-year All-American plugging the middle for the vaunted Vol defense.

1928

TENNESSEE 15, ALABAMA 13

Tennessee and Alabama hadn't played each other for fourteen years, and the Crimson Tide had won eight of the previous eleven meetings. But this was the first with Bob Neyland at the helm for the Volunteers. Neyland's first two teams had posted records of 8–1 and 8–0–1, an accomplishment scarcely known outside of Knoxville. The Volunteers needed a win over somebody big, and nobody was bigger than Alabama, which was coming off consecutive Rose Bowl trips under coach Wallace Wade. Tennessee sophomore halfback Gene McEver's 98-yard touchdown on the opening kickoff opened the festivities, and the Vols won the game 15–13. The win focused national attention on Tennessee and its "Hack, Mack and Dodd" backfield of Buddy Hackman, McEver and Bobby Dodd.

1939 ORANGE BOWL

TENNESSEE 17, OKLAHOMA 0

Tennessee finished the 1938 regular season 10–0 and ranked second in the nation behind TCU and Heisman Trophy winner Davey O'Brien. The Vols' first-ever bowl game — in the Orange Bowl against fourth-ranked Oklahoma — ensued. The

Sooners were also 10–0, and had won their last fourteen games. The game was billed as one of speed (Tennessee) versus power (Oklahoma). Speed won. It is remembered as one of the most vicious football games ever played. One journalist referred to the contest as the "Orange Brawl." Players were knocked out of the game with startling regularity. A block by Tennessee All-American George Cafego finished OU All-American Waddy Young for the day. UT center Joe Little was ejected from the game for retaliating after a Sooner cheap shot. Touchdowns by Bob Foxx and Babe Wood, a Bowden Wyatt field goal, and a shutout by a typically impenetrable Neyland defense, rendered a final tally of 17–0.

1950
TENNESSEE 7, KENTUCKY 0

Many observers felt the 1950 Tennessee team was superior to its 1951 National Champions. After dropping Game 2 to Mississippi State, the '50 Vols rolled over seven straight opponents before their matchup with Bear Bryant's undefeated, top-ranked Kentucky team. The Wildcats, led by Southeastern Conference MVP Babe Parilli at quarterback, had already clinched the SEC crown. The Vols weren't given much of a chance entering the contest, but their defense, spearheaded by Bill Pearman, Ted Daffer, Bud Sherrod and Doug Atkins, kept Parilli on the run most of the day. A 27-yard touchdown pass from Hank Lauricella to Bert Rechichar was all the scoring the Big Orange needed.

1951 COTTON BOWL
TENNESSEE 20, TEXAS 14

Had the final polls been taken after the postseason in 1950 as they are today, Tennessee would have been National Champion. Neyland's Vols, 10–1 and ranked fourth nationally, traveled to Dallas to take on the 9–1, third-ranked Texas Longhorns on New Year's Day, 1951. The Volunteers scored first on a short pass from Herky Payne to John Gruble. The score was set up by a memorable 75-yard run by All-American Hank Lauricella. The Horns stormed back to lead 14–7 at intermission, but the Vols owned the second half. Neyland's troops, using the single wing formation that had been ditched by all but one or two other teams in favor of the T-Formation, stormed back for 13 fourth-quarter points on a pair of touchdown plunges by fullback Andy Kozar. Tennessee's speed won over Texas' bulk to the tune of a 20–14 final score. With top-ranked Oklahoma falling to Kentucky in the Sugar Bowl that same day, a post-bowl poll would have crowned Tennessee champion.

1956
TENNESSEE 6, GEORGIA TECH 0

In 1956, Bowden Wyatt enjoyed the best campaign of his eight-year coaching regime in Knoxville. Tennessee and then-SEC foe Georgia Tech, coached by former UT Vol Bobby Dodd, were each 6–0 entering their classic matchup. Wyatt and Dodd had both trained as players under Neyland, and now they coached the two finest teams in the Southeastern Conference. A pair of third-quarter passes from Johnny Majors to Buddy Cruze set up the game's only score, a one-yard plunge by Tommy Bronson. The Vols held on for the win in what was to be Tech's only loss of the season.

1959
TENNESSEE 14, LSU 13

In 1959, LSU was the defending National Champion with Paul Dietzel as coach and Heisman Trophy winner Billy Cannon as its star halfback. The Bayou Bengals brought a nineteen-game winning streak and No. 1 ranking into Knoxville on November 7 to face the 4–1–1 Vols. Cannon and Johnny Robinson ran wild in the first half for LSU, but the Tigers could only manage to squeeze out seven points by halftime. In the third period, Tennessee's Jim Cartwright intercepted a Warren Rabb pass and returned it 59 yards for a game-tying touchdown. The Vols took a 14–7 lead on a 14-yard Neyle Sollee run. A fumbled punt at the 2-yard line led to LSU's final touchdown and brought the score to 14–13. But Cannon was stopped short on the two-point conversion try in one of the greatest moments in Tennessee football history, preserving the huge upset win.

1986 SUGAR BOWL
TENNESSEE 35, MIAMI 7

Miami finished the 1985 regular season on a ten-game winning streak, having not lost since dropping its opener to Florida 35–23. Coach Jimmy Johnson brought his Hurricanes into the Sugar Bowl to face Johnny Majors' SEC Champion Tennessee squad. The Canes took a 7–0 lead on an 18-yard pass from Vinny Testaverde to Michael Irvin to end the first quarter, but after that it was all UT. A six-yard touchdown pass from Daryl Dickey to Jeff Smith in the second quarter knotted the score at 7–7 and sent the game spiraling out of Miami's control. The Vols led 14–7 at the half, tacked on two more TDs in the third period, including a 60-yard punt return by Jeff Powell, and another in the fourth. The defense produced seven sacks and six turnovers, sending the highly partisan crowd into a frenzy that spilled onto Bourbon Street. The final tally: Tennessee 35, Miami 7. It was the resounding exclamation point on one of the truly magical seasons in Tennessee history.

1991

It was the greatest come-from-behind win in Tennessee history and the greatest comeback ever at Notre Dame Stadium. On November 9, 1991, at South Bend, Notre Dame jumped out to a 21–0 first-quarter lead, and led 31–7 in the second quarter. Just before halftime, Darryl Hardy blocked a field goal attempt by ND's Craig Hentrich. Floyd Miley scooped up the ball and took off on an 85-yard touchdown jaunt to bring the score to 31–14 at intermission. The Volunteers scored three TDs in the second half, including two by Aaron Hayden, to take the lead 35–34. Irish walk-on kicker Rob Leonard, subbing for an injured Hentrich, came in for a 27-yard field goal as time expired, but Jeremy Lincoln blocked the attempt and the Vols came away winners.

1998

Tennessee's 34–33 win over Syracuse in the 1998 season opener could qualify for greatest-game status, but it was the Vols' next game, two weeks later against Florida, that fans remember most fondly. After a Florida field goal, Shawn Bryson scored on a 57-yard run for a 7–3 Tennessee lead in the first quarter. The first half ended in a 10–10 deadlock. After three quarters the score was knotted at 17, and the final period was scoreless. Jeff Hall kicked a 41-yard field goal in the first-ever overtime period for both schools, and UT led 20–17. Jeff Chandler came up empty on his 32-yard attempt to end the Gators' overtime possession, and the Vols were off and running to a National Title. Deon Grant's fourth-quarter interception and linebacker Al Wilson's nine tackles and school-record three forced fumbles were keys to the win. And the Neyland Stadium goal-post enjoyed a late-night parade through the strip as Knoxville celebrated like never before.

THE ARTFUL DODGER

Condredge Holloway's artistic escape acts became legendary during the little quarterback's tenure at Tennessee and resulted in some memorable victories. But the most remarkable performance by the man they called the Artful Dodger may have come in a game the Volunteers didn't win. In the 1974 season opener against UCLA, Holloway led Tennessee to a 10–0 first-quarter lead before injuring his shoulder. Holloway was rushed to a nearby hospital for X-rays, which proved negative. Returning to Neyland Stadium to deafening roars, Holloway re-entered the game over the objections of coach Bill Battle. With Tennessee facing a 17–10 deficit, the Huntsville Houdini rallied the Vols to a tying touchdown, leaping over defenders into the end zone at the end of a 12-yard fourth-quarter run.

"I'M GOING TO STAY..."

When Peyton Manning walked to the podium for a press conference in March 1997, many were prepared for the worst. Manning had rewritten the Tennessee record books during his three years as the unofficial president of Vol Nation, and the riches of professional football that were seemingly his birthright beckoned him to leave The Hill after his junior season.

But Manning, the type of kid for whom the phrase "student-athlete" was seemingly coined, had other ideas. The following nine-word statement thrilled fans all across Rocky Top, while stunning others who were certain he was leaving:

"I'm going to stay at the University of Tennessee."

The packed house erupted, as fellow players, media, athletic department officials, friends and family reveled in the news. "I've had an incredible experience at the University of Tennessee with all the people I've met, learned from, and become friends with here," Manning explained. "College football has been great to me, so have the people, and the coaches and players I've played with the past three years. I wanted to come back and be a college student one more year and enjoy the entire experience."

Said coach Phillip Fulmer: "Today we are blessed with the ultimate return of loyalty and commitment . . . Peyton's decision makes a huge statement, I think, for Peyton Manning and his character, putting team and program and alumni and fans and friends and teammates ahead of immediate financial gains and the limelight of the National Football League."

THE THIRD SATURDAY IN OCTOBER
TENNESSEE VS. ALABAMA

For now, Florida fills the role of preeminent Tennessee rival. For a time, beating Auburn was the ultimate prize for Tennessee fans. But for history and enduring intensity, nothing can match the spectacle that is Tennessee vs. Alabama.

On October 20, 1928, in one swift and sudden moment, one of the greatest of all college football rivalries was born: Tennessee versus Alabama. Sophomore halfback Gene McEver returned Alabama's opening kickoff 98 yards for the touchdown that detonated Tennessee's monumental upset victory, 15–13. Football historians agree that Tennessee football came of age with that 1928 triumph over Alabama.

NO TEAM HAD EVER BEATEN ALABAMA SEVEN YEARS IN A ROW UNTIL TENNESSEE STRUNG TOGETHER SEVEN STRAIGHT FROM 1995–2001.

The 1939 game, a 21–0 UT win at Knoxville, is remembered for one of the most spectacular plays in the history of Southern football. Tennessee sophomore tailback Johnny Butler zigzagged his way through the entire Alabama team—left, right and then left again—en route to a 56-yard touchdown.

Recent decades have seen one team or the other string together long winning streaks in the series. The most maddening for Vol fans, an 11-year Alabama run, came to an end in 1982 when quarterback Alan Cockrell and receiver Willie Gault led Tennessee to a 35–28 upset victory. An end zone interception by defensive end Mike Terry put down a furious Bama rally to secure the win.

No team had ever beaten Alabama seven years in a row until Tennessee strung together seven straight from 1995–2001.

TALKING
TENNESSEE FOOTBALL

"Mr. Speaker, I have often said that in my district, the colors orange and white are almost as patriotic as red, white, and blue. That is because orange and white represents the official colors of the University of Tennessee and the Tennessee Volunteers football team, now the undisputed NCAA national football champion.

"Mr. Speaker, just a few short weeks ago the Tennessee Vols completed a perfect 13–0 season and earned their first national championship in 47 years.

"Mr. Speaker, I congratulate the newly crowned NCAA National Champion Tennessee Volunteers and everyone who has contributed to their perfect season. Go Vols!"

EXCERPTS FROM REMARKS MADE BY TENNESSEE CONGRESSMAN JOHN DUNCAN, ON THE FLOOR OF THE UNITED STATES HOUSE OF REPRESENTATIVES, JAN. 19, 1999

"Tennessee definitely has one of the best fan bases in all of football, and they travel with as many fans as anyone in the country. There are only a few schools that can compete with Vol fans; teams like Nebraska and some SEC schools travel like Tennessee, but not many. Then again I don't think you could ever hope to have any more support as a Tennessee player, from the fans that UT brings game after game. It really is amazing."

FORMER TENNESSEE OFFENSIVE TACKLE TREY TEAGUE, TO THE *JACKSON SUN*

"I'LL BE A TENNESSEE VOLUNTEER FOR THE REST OF MY LIFE."

PEYTON MANNING

"People are waiting for Tennessee to mess up, but I've got another story for them. We're not going to mess up. We have something to prove. We're on a mission."

CO-CAPTAIN AL WILSON, DURING THE 1998 NATIONAL CHAMPIONSHIP SEASON

BOWL GAME TRADITION

1939 Orange Bowl	Tennessee 17, Oklahoma 0
1940 Rose Bowl	Southern Cal 14, Tennessee 0
1941 Sugar Bowl	Boston College 19, Tennessee 13
1943 Sugar Bowl	Tennessee 14, Tulsa 7
1945 Rose Bowl	Southern Cal 25, Tennessee 0
1947 Orange Bowl	Rice 8, Tennessee 0
1951 Cotton Bowl	Tennessee 20, Texas 14
1952 Sugar Bowl	Maryland 28, Tennessee 13
1953 Cotton Bowl	Texas 16, Tennessee 0
1957 Sugar Bowl	Baylor 13, Tennessee 7
1957 Gator Bowl	Tennessee 3, Texas A&M 0
1965 Bluebonnet Bowl	Tennessee 27, Tulsa 6
1966 Gator Bowl	Tennessee 18, Syracuse 12
1968 Orange Bowl	Oklahoma 26, Tennessee 24
1969 Cotton Bowl	Texas 36, Tennessee 13
1969 Gator Bowl	Florida 14, Tennessee 13
1971 Sugar Bowl	Tennessee 34, Air Force 13
1971 Liberty Bowl	Tennessee 14, Arkansas 13

1972 Bluebonnet Bowl	Tennessee 24, LSU 17
1973 Gator Bowl	Texas Tech 28, Tennessee 19
1974 Liberty Bowl	Tennessee 7, Maryland 3
1979 Bluebonnet Bowl	Purdue 27, Tennessee 22
1981 Garden State Bowl	Tennessee 28, Wisconsin 21
1982 Peach Bowl	Iowa 28, Tennessee 22
1983 Florida Citrus Bowl	Tennessee 30, Maryland 23
1984 Sun Bowl	Maryland 28, Tennessee 27
1986 Sugar Bowl	Tennessee 35, Miami 7
1986 Liberty Bowl	Tennessee 21, Minnesota 14
1988 Peach Bowl	Tennessee 27, Indiana 22
1990 Cotton Bowl	Tennessee 31, Arkansas 27
1991 Sugar Bowl	Tennessee 23, Virginia 22
1992 Fiesta Bowl	Penn State 42, Tennessee 17
1993 Hall of Fame Bowl	Tennessee 38, Boston College 23
1994 Florida Citrus Bowl	Penn State 31, Tennessee 13
1994 Gator Bowl	Tennessee 45, Virginia Tech 23
1996 Florida Citrus Bowl	Tennessee 20, Ohio State 14
1997 Florida Citrus Bowl	Tennessee 48, Northwestern 28
1998 Orange Bowl	Nebraska 42, Tennessee 17
1999 Fiesta Bowl	Tennessee 23, Florida State 16
2000 Fiesta Bowl	Nebraska 31, Tennessee 21
2001 Cotton Bowl	Kansas State 35, Tennessee 21
2002 Florida Citrus Bowl	Tennessee 45, Michigan 17
2002 Peach Bowl	Maryland 30, Tennessee 3